SAVING ANIMALS FROM THE BRINK

FUR-TASTROPHE AVOIDED

SOUTHERN SEA OTTER COMEBACK

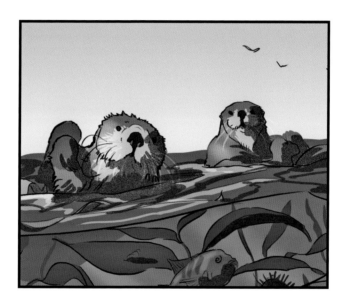

BY TIM COOKE
ILLUSTRATED BY ALESSANDRO VALDRIGHI

BEARPORT PUBLISHING

Minneapolis, Minnesota

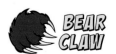

BEAR CLAW

Credits: 20, © Chonlasub Woravichan/Shutterstock; 21, © Chase Dekker/Shutterstock; 22t, © Andrew Sutton/Shutterstock; 22b, © Lorraine Logan/Shutterstock.

Editor: Sarah Eason
Proofreader: Harriet McGregor
Designers: Jessica Moon and Steve Mead
Picture Researcher: Rachel Blount

DISCLAIMER: This graphic story is a dramatization based on true events. It is intended to give the reader a sense of the narrative rather than a presentation of actual details as they occurred.

Library of Congress Cataloging-in-Publication Data

Names: Cooke, Tim, 1961- author. | Valdrighi, Alessandro, illustrator.
Title: Fur-tastrophe avoided : southern sea otter comeback / by Tim Cooke ;
   illustrated by Alessandro Valdrighi.
Description: Bear claw books edition. | Minneapolis, Minnesota : Bearport
   Publishing Company, [2022] | Series: Saving animals from the brink |
   Includes bibliographical references and index.
Identifiers: LCCN 2020057400 (print) | LCCN 2020057401 (ebook) | ISBN
   9781636910482 (library binding) | ISBN 9781636910550 (paperback) | ISBN
   9781636910628 (ebook)
Subjects: LCSH: Sharpe, Howard Granville--Juvenile literature. | Sea
   otter--Conservation--California--Juvenile literature. |
   Conservationists--United States--Juvenile literature.
Classification: LCC QL737.C25 C6765 2022 (print) | LCC QL737.C25 (ebook)
   | DDC 599.769/509794--dc23
LC record available at https://lccn.loc.gov/2020057400
LC ebook record available at https://lccn.loc.gov/2020057401

For more information, write to Bearport Publishing, 5357 Penn Avenue South, Minneapolis, MN 55419. Printed in the United States of America.

CONTENTS

Chapter 1

An Amazing Discovery 4

Chapter 2

Helping the Otters 8

Chapter 3

Protect the Otters! 14

Southern Sea Otter Facts 20

Other Marine Mammals in Danger 22

Glossary 23

Index 24

Read More 24

Learn More Online 24

CHAPTER 1

AN AMAZING DISCOVERY

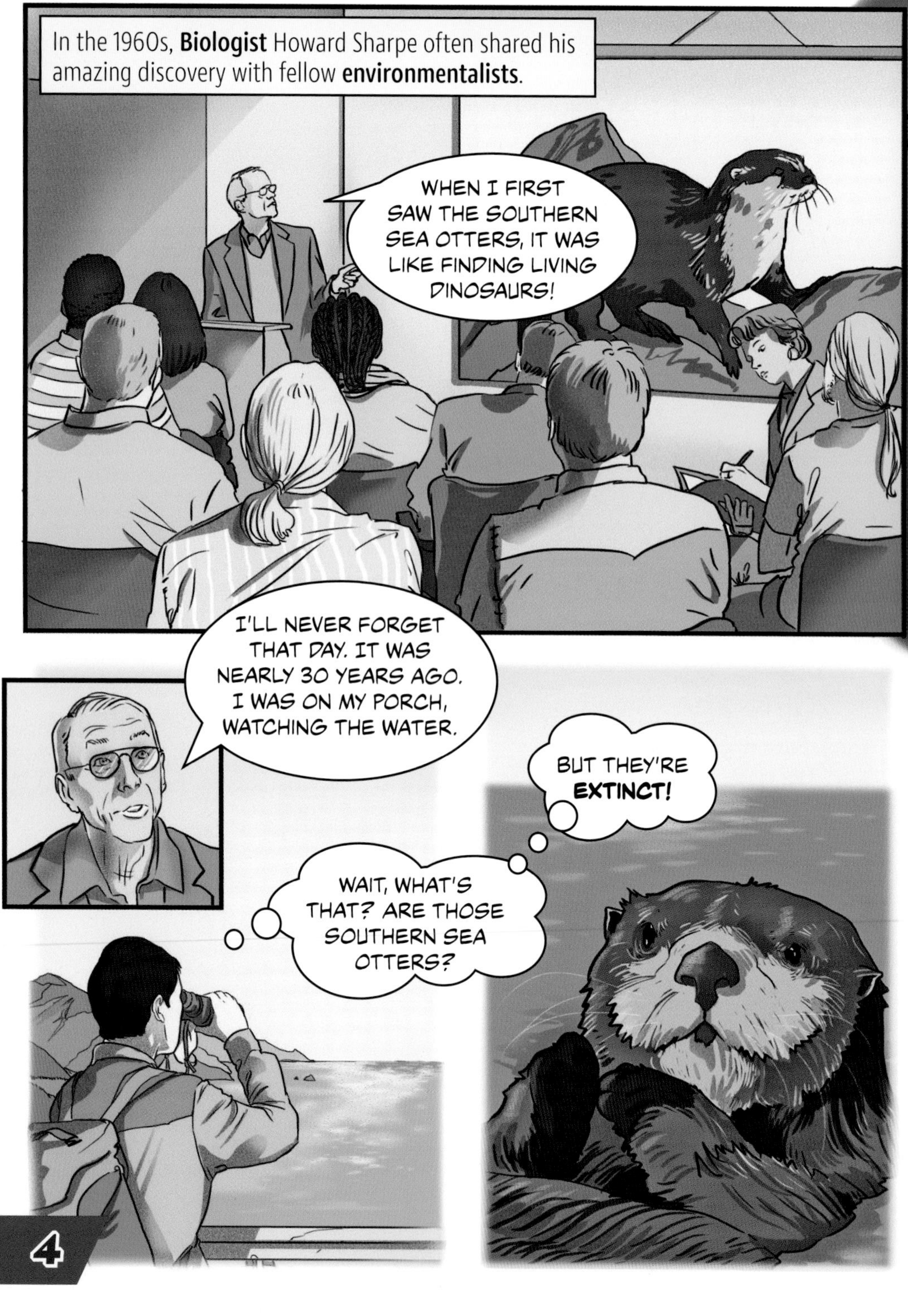

In the 1960s, **Biologist** Howard Sharpe often shared his amazing discovery with fellow **environmentalists**.
WHEN I FIRST SAW THE SOUTHERN SEA OTTERS, IT WAS LIKE FINDING LIVING DINOSAURS!
I'LL NEVER FORGET THAT DAY. IT WAS NEARLY 30 YEARS AGO. I WAS ON MY PORCH, WATCHING THE WATER.
WAIT, WHAT'S THAT? ARE THOSE SOUTHERN SEA OTTERS?
BUT THEY'RE **EXTINCT!**

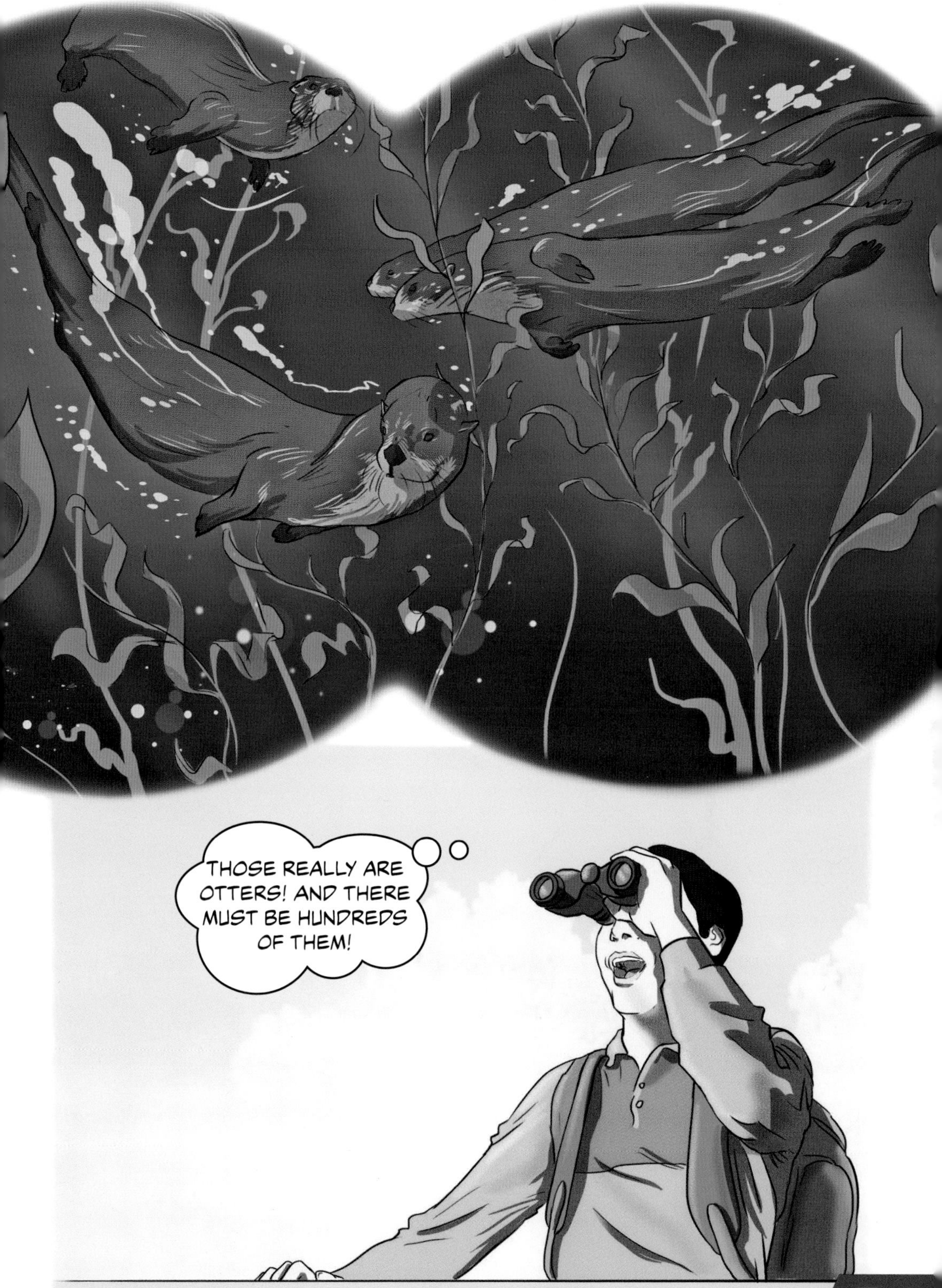
THOSE REALLY ARE OTTERS! AND THERE MUST BE HUNDREDS OF THEM!

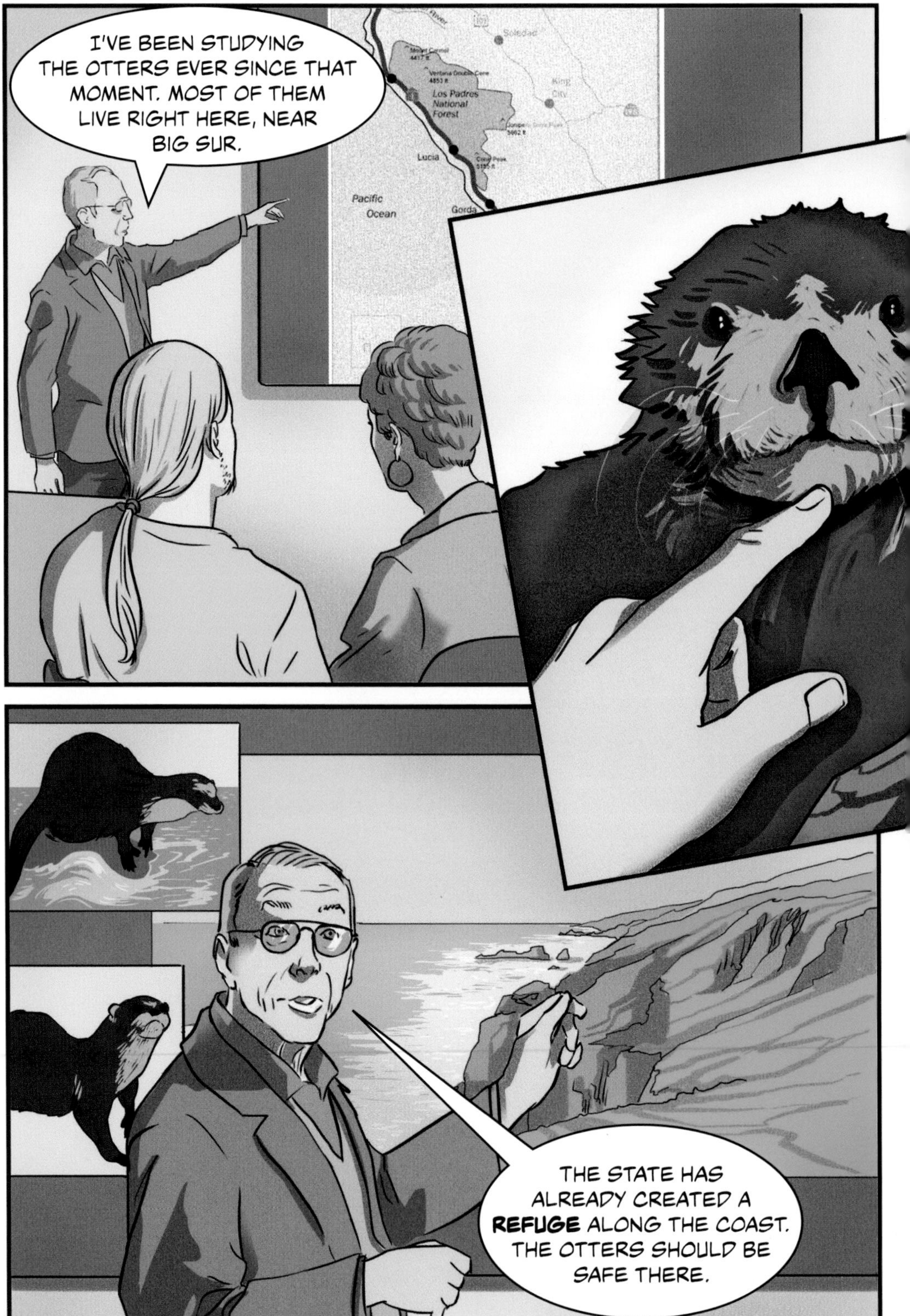
I'VE BEEN STUDYING THE OTTERS EVER SINCE THAT MOMENT. MOST OF THEM LIVE RIGHT HERE, NEAR BIG SUR.
Soledad
King City
Los Padres National Forest
Lucia
Pacific Ocean
Gorda
THE STATE HAS ALREADY CREATED A **REFUGE** ALONG THE COAST. THE OTTERS SHOULD BE SAFE THERE.

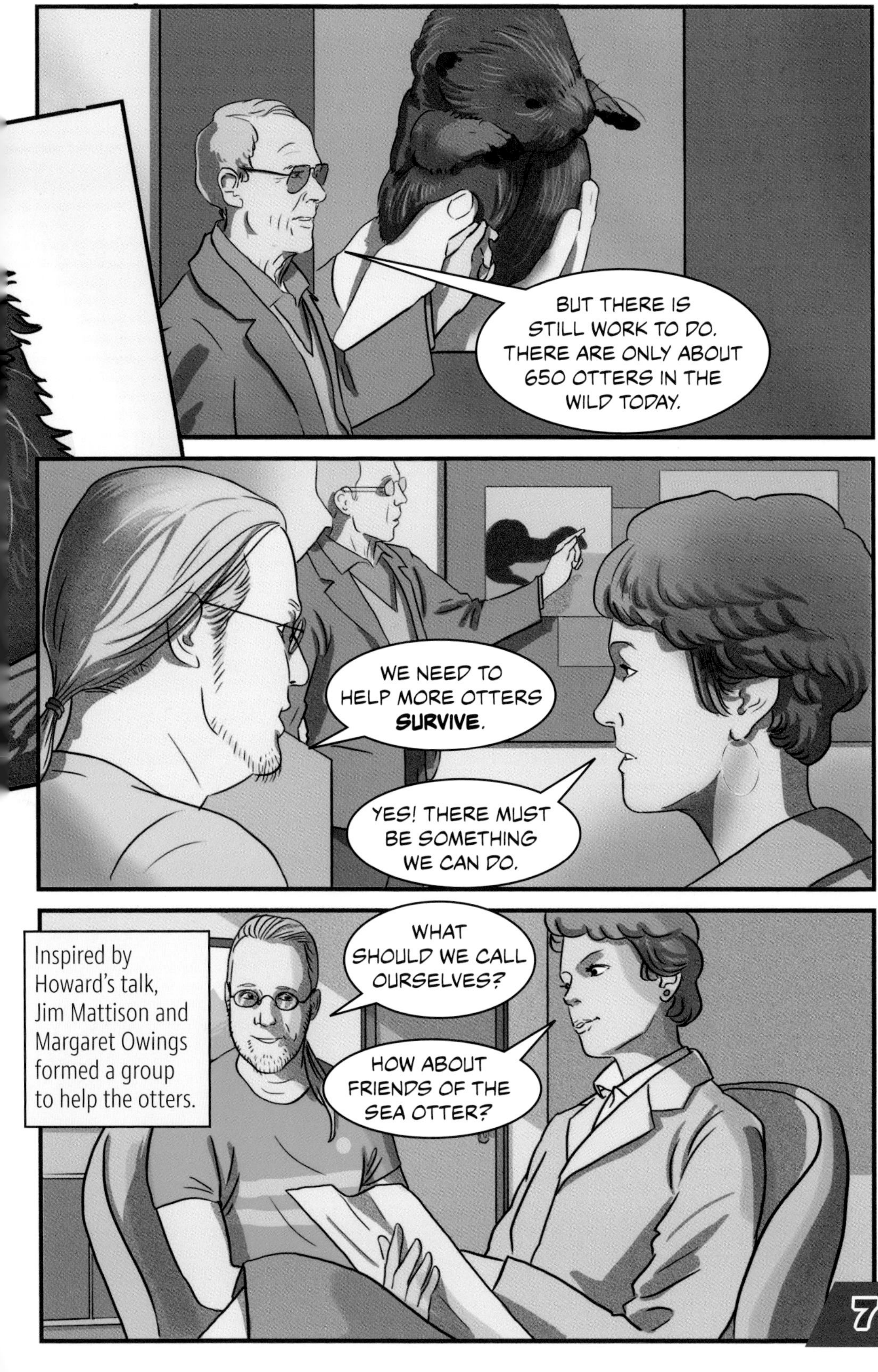
BUT THERE IS STILL WORK TO DO. THERE ARE ONLY ABOUT 650 OTTERS IN THE WILD TODAY.
WE NEED TO HELP MORE OTTERS **SURVIVE**.
YES! THERE MUST BE SOMETHING WE CAN DO.
Inspired by Howard's talk, Jim Mattison and Margaret Owings formed a group to help the otters.
WHAT SHOULD WE CALL OURSELVES?
HOW ABOUT FRIENDS OF THE SEA OTTER?

CHAPTER 2

HELPING THE OTTERS

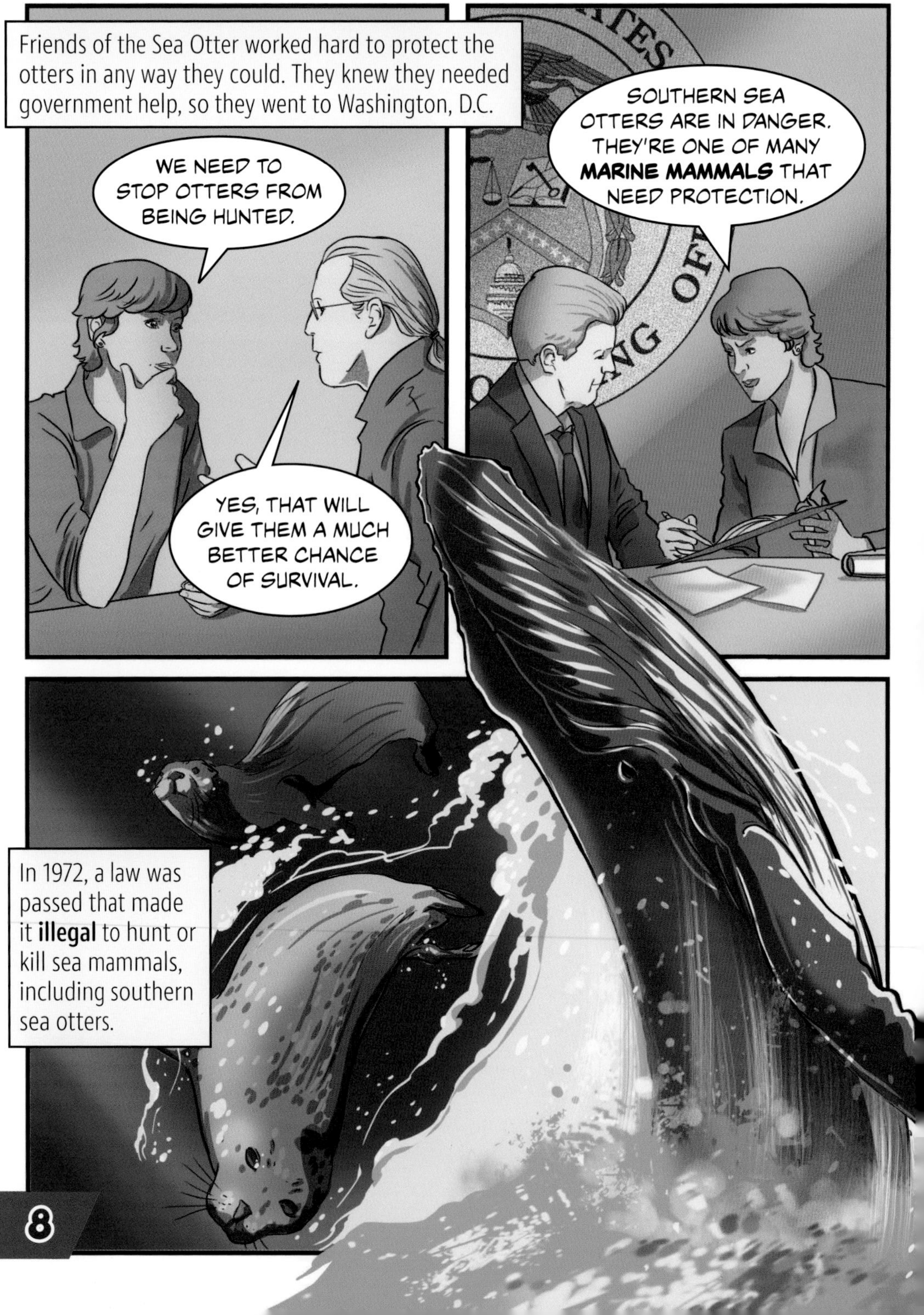
Friends of the Sea Otter worked hard to protect the otters in any way they could. They knew they needed government help, so they went to Washington, D.C.
WE NEED TO STOP OTTERS FROM BEING HUNTED.
YES, THAT WILL GIVE THEM A MUCH BETTER CHANCE OF SURVIVAL.
SOUTHERN SEA OTTERS ARE IN DANGER. THEY'RE ONE OF MANY **MARINE MAMMALS** THAT NEED PROTECTION.
In 1972, a law was passed that made it **illegal** to hunt or kill sea mammals, including southern sea otters.

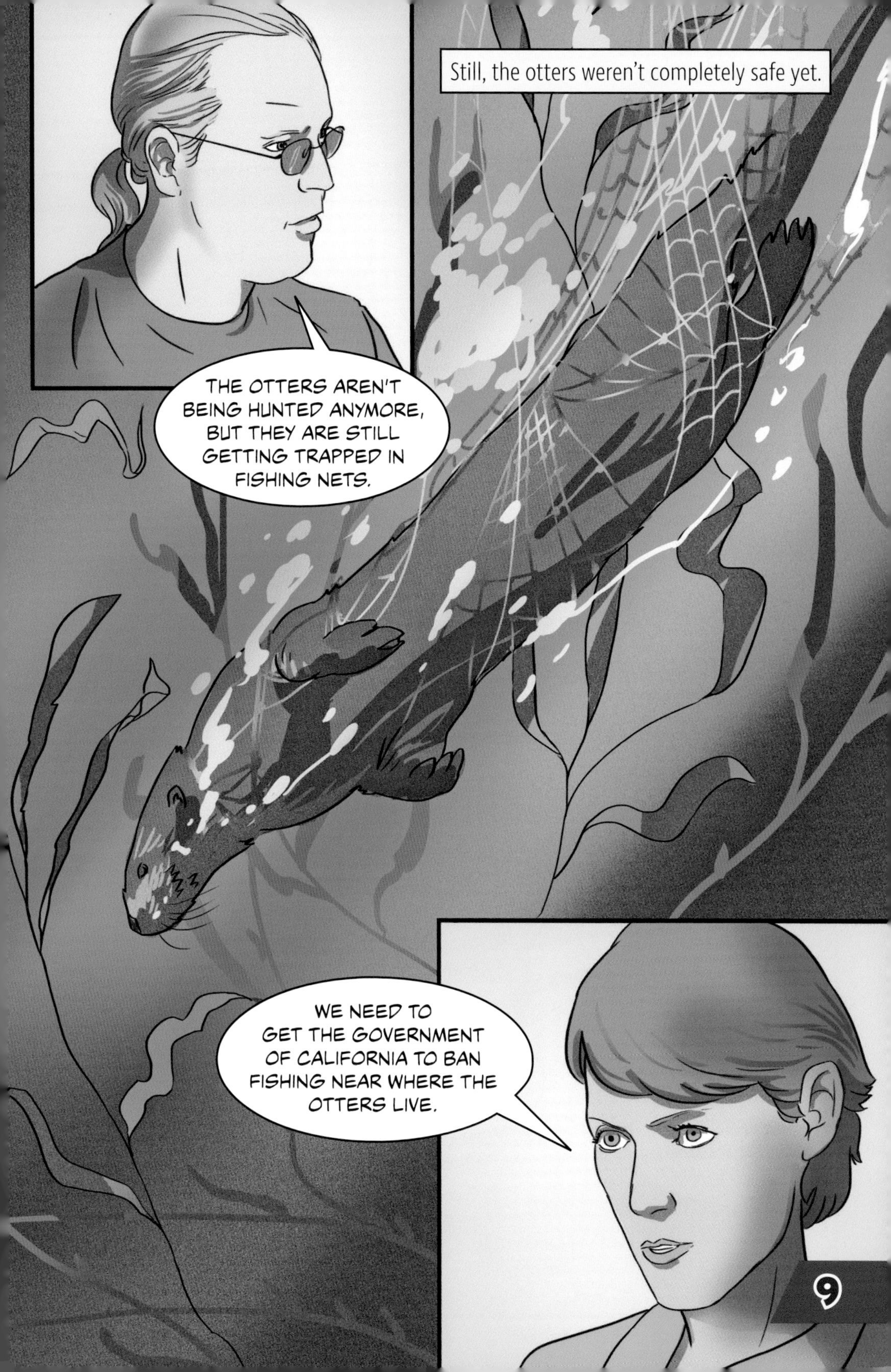
Still, the otters weren't completely safe yet.
THE OTTERS AREN'T BEING HUNTED ANYMORE, BUT THEY ARE STILL GETTING TRAPPED IN FISHING NETS.
WE NEED TO GET THE GOVERNMENT OF CALIFORNIA TO BAN FISHING NEAR WHERE THE OTTERS LIVE.

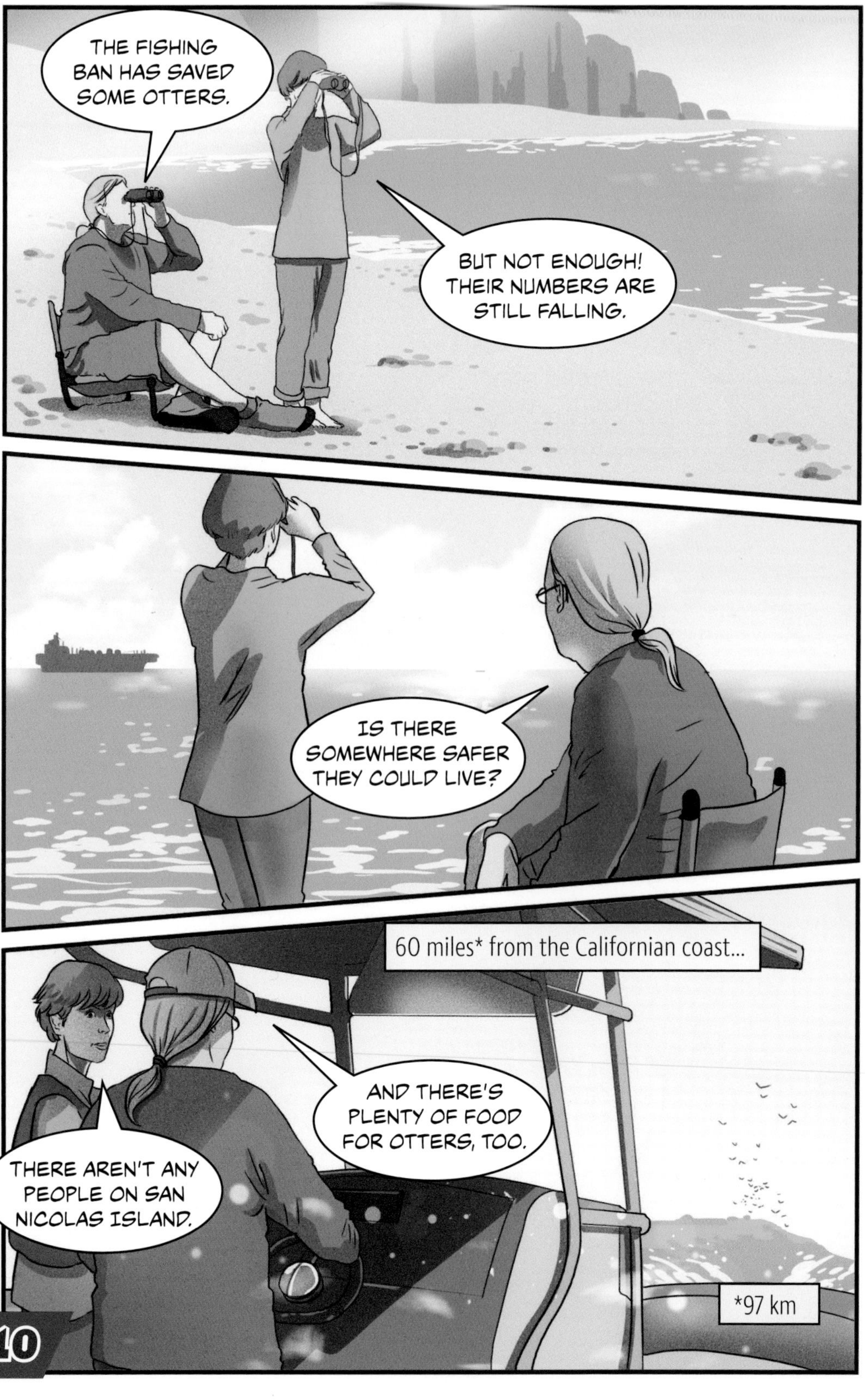
THE FISHING BAN HAS SAVED SOME OTTERS.
BUT NOT ENOUGH! THEIR NUMBERS ARE STILL FALLING.
IS THERE SOMEWHERE SAFER THEY COULD LIVE?
60 miles* from the Californian coast...
THERE AREN'T ANY PEOPLE ON SAN NICOLAS ISLAND.
AND THERE'S PLENTY OF FOOD FOR OTTERS, TOO.
*97 km

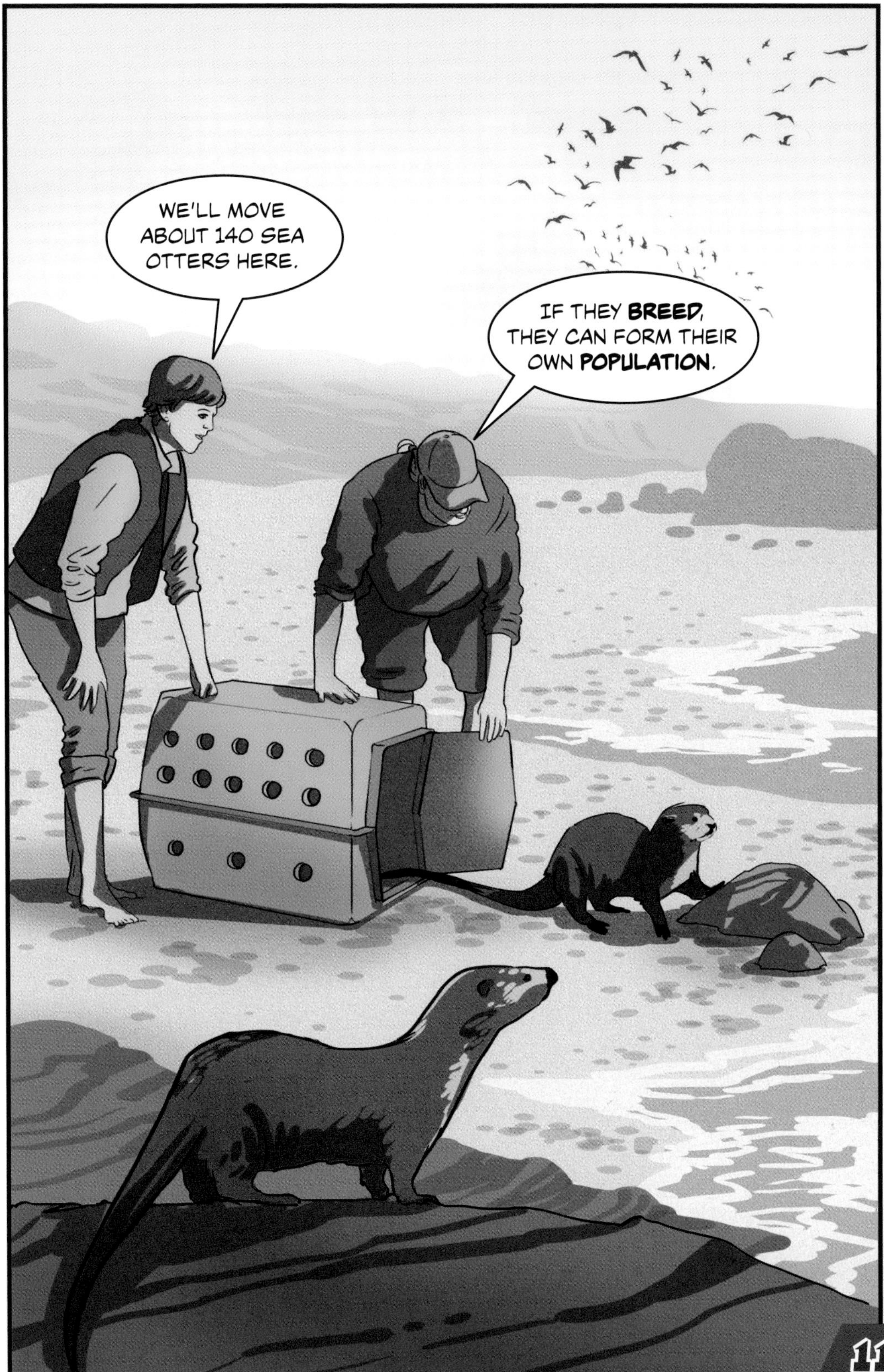
WE'LL MOVE ABOUT 140 SEA OTTERS HERE.
IF THEY **BREED**, THEY CAN FORM THEIR OWN **POPULATION**.

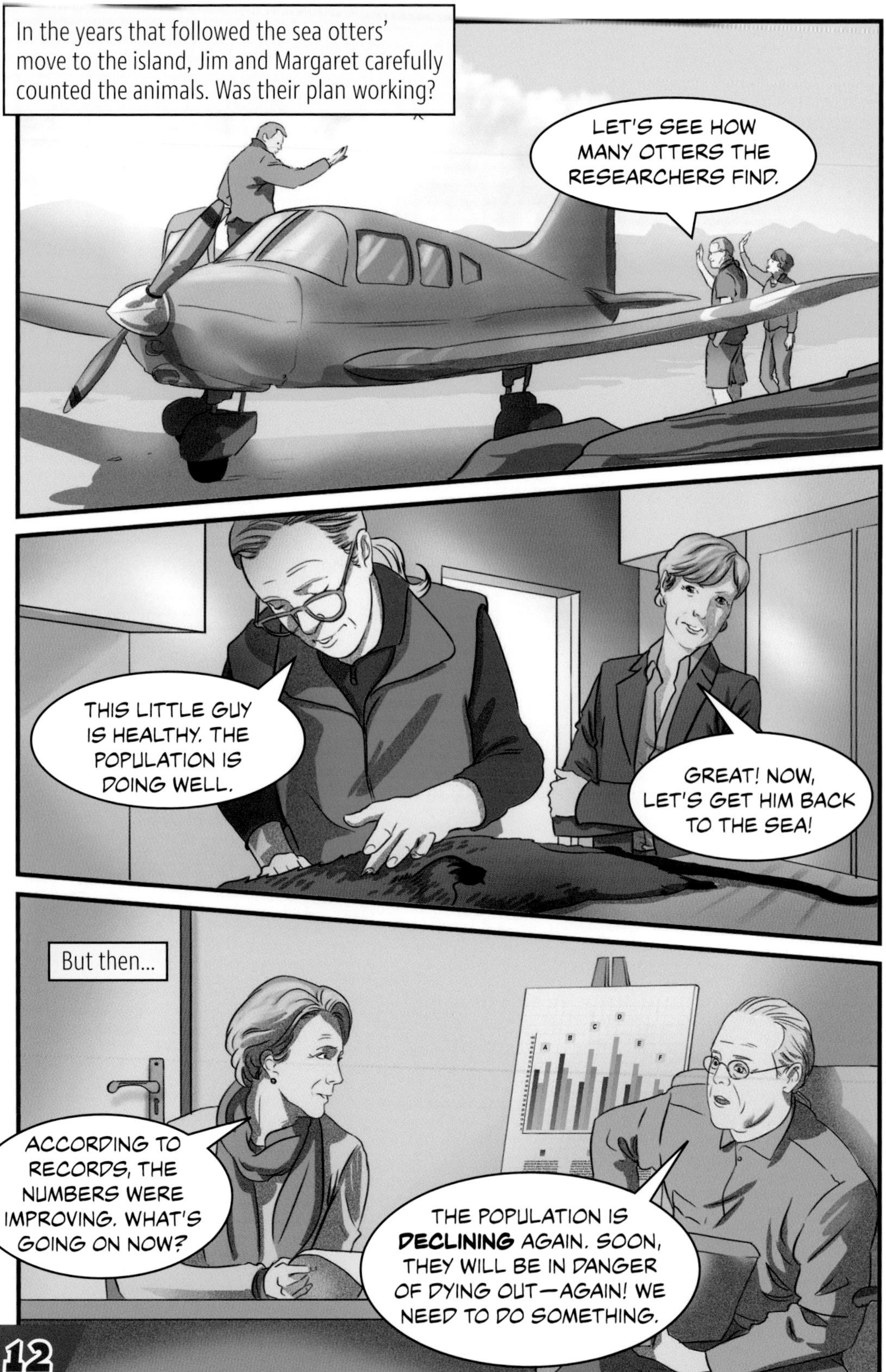
In the years that followed the sea otters' move to the island, Jim and Margaret carefully counted the animals. Was their plan working?
LET'S SEE HOW MANY OTTERS THE RESEARCHERS FIND.
THIS LITTLE GUY IS HEALTHY. THE POPULATION IS DOING WELL.
GREAT! NOW, LET'S GET HIM BACK TO THE SEA!
But then...
ACCORDING TO RECORDS, THE NUMBERS WERE IMPROVING. WHAT'S GOING ON NOW?
THE POPULATION IS **DECLINING** AGAIN. SOON, THEY WILL BE IN DANGER OF DYING OUT—AGAIN! WE NEED TO DO SOMETHING.

Why was Friends of the Sea Otter so worried? The southern sea otters were a **keystone species**. This means they were important to all the living things in their **habitat**.

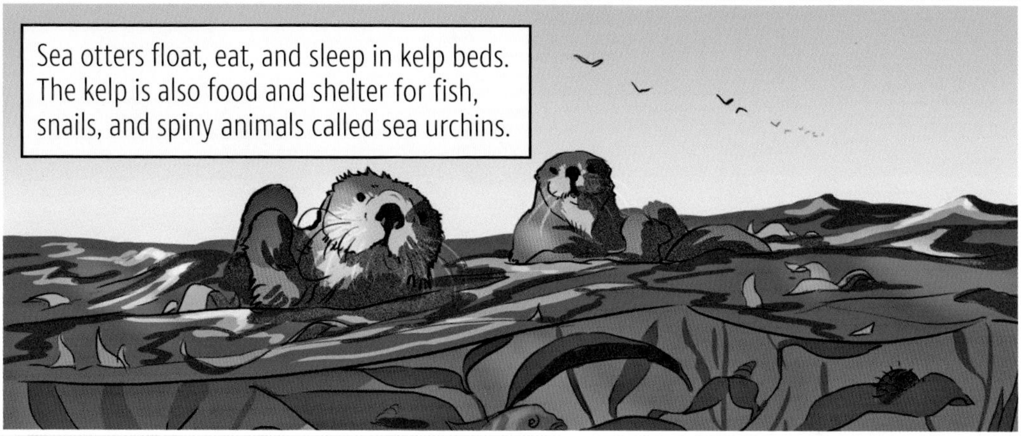
Sea otters float, eat, and sleep in kelp beds. The kelp is also food and shelter for fish, snails, and spiny animals called sea urchins.

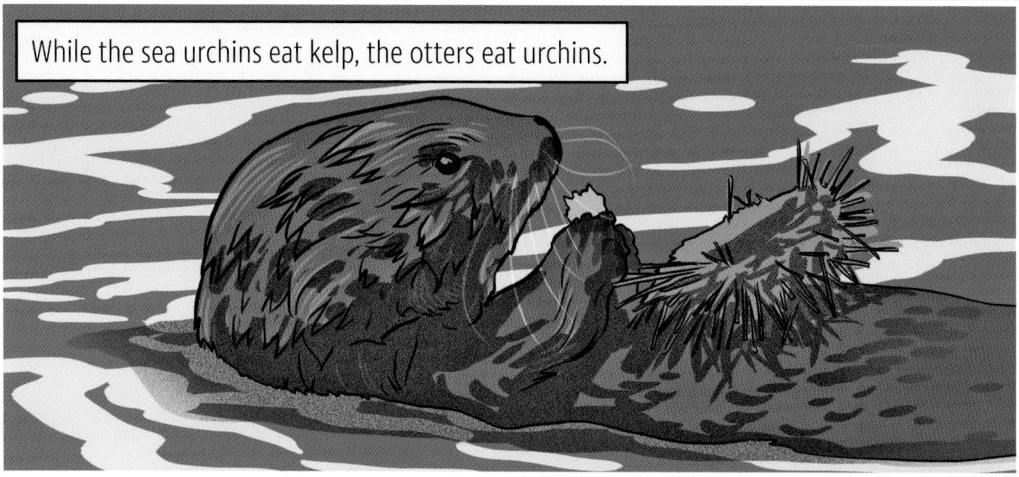
While the sea urchins eat kelp, the otters eat urchins.

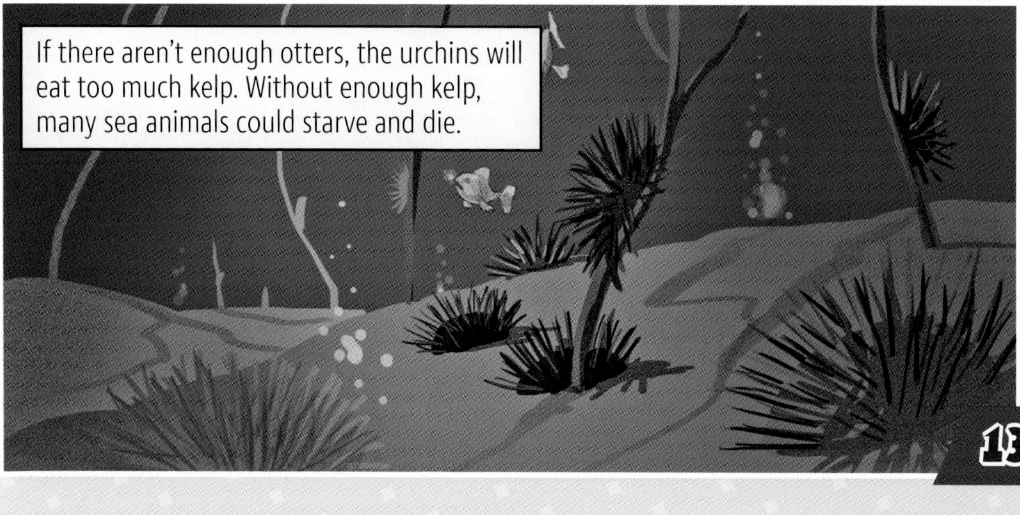
If there aren't enough otters, the urchins will eat too much kelp. Without enough kelp, many sea animals could starve and die.

CHAPTER 3

PROTECT THE OTTERS!

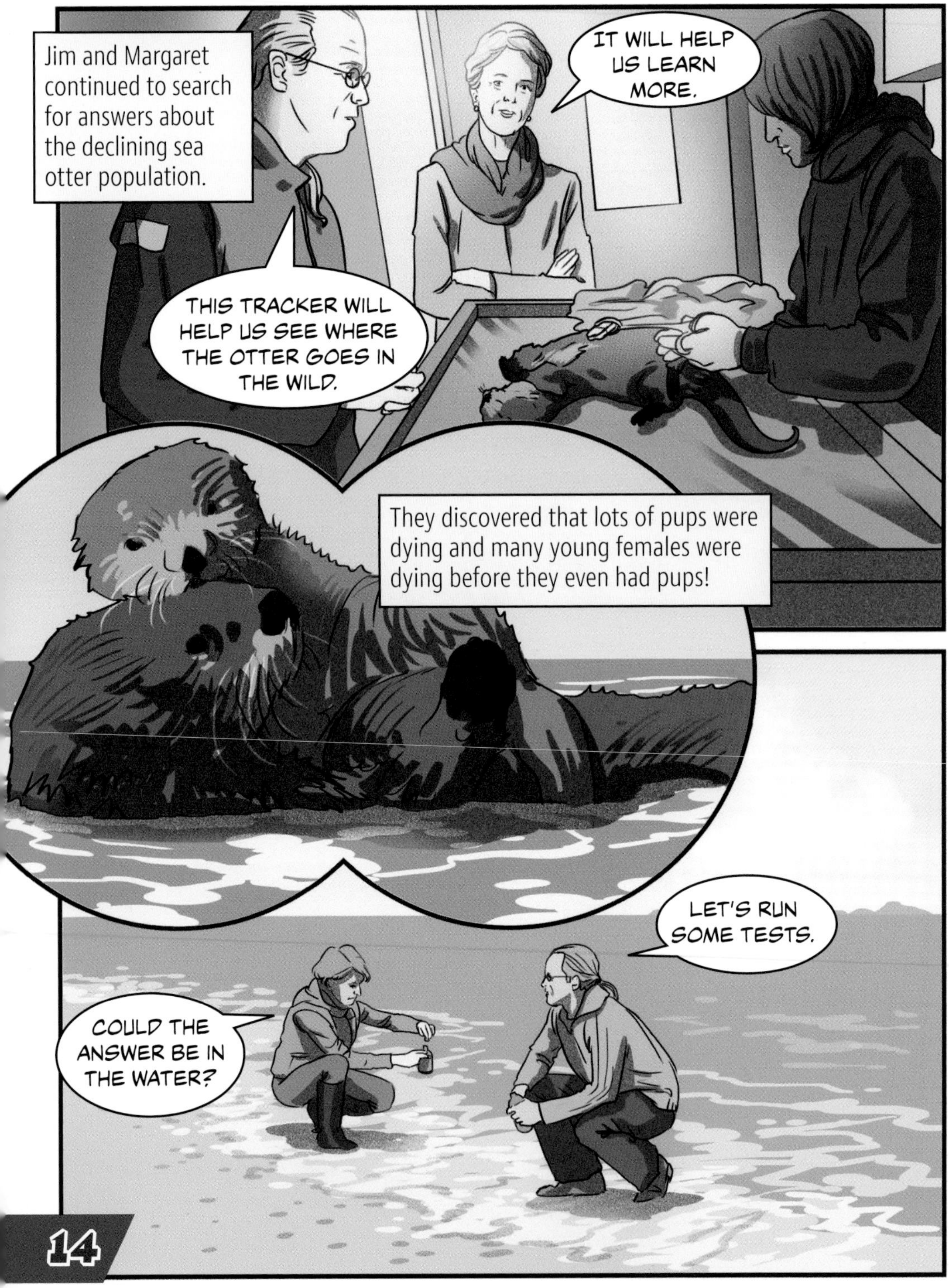
Jim and Margaret continued to search for answers about the declining sea otter population.
IT WILL HELP US LEARN MORE.
THIS TRACKER WILL HELP US SEE WHERE THE OTTER GOES IN THE WILD.
They discovered that lots of pups were dying and many young females were dying before they even had pups!
LET'S RUN SOME TESTS.
COULD THE ANSWER BE IN THE WATER?

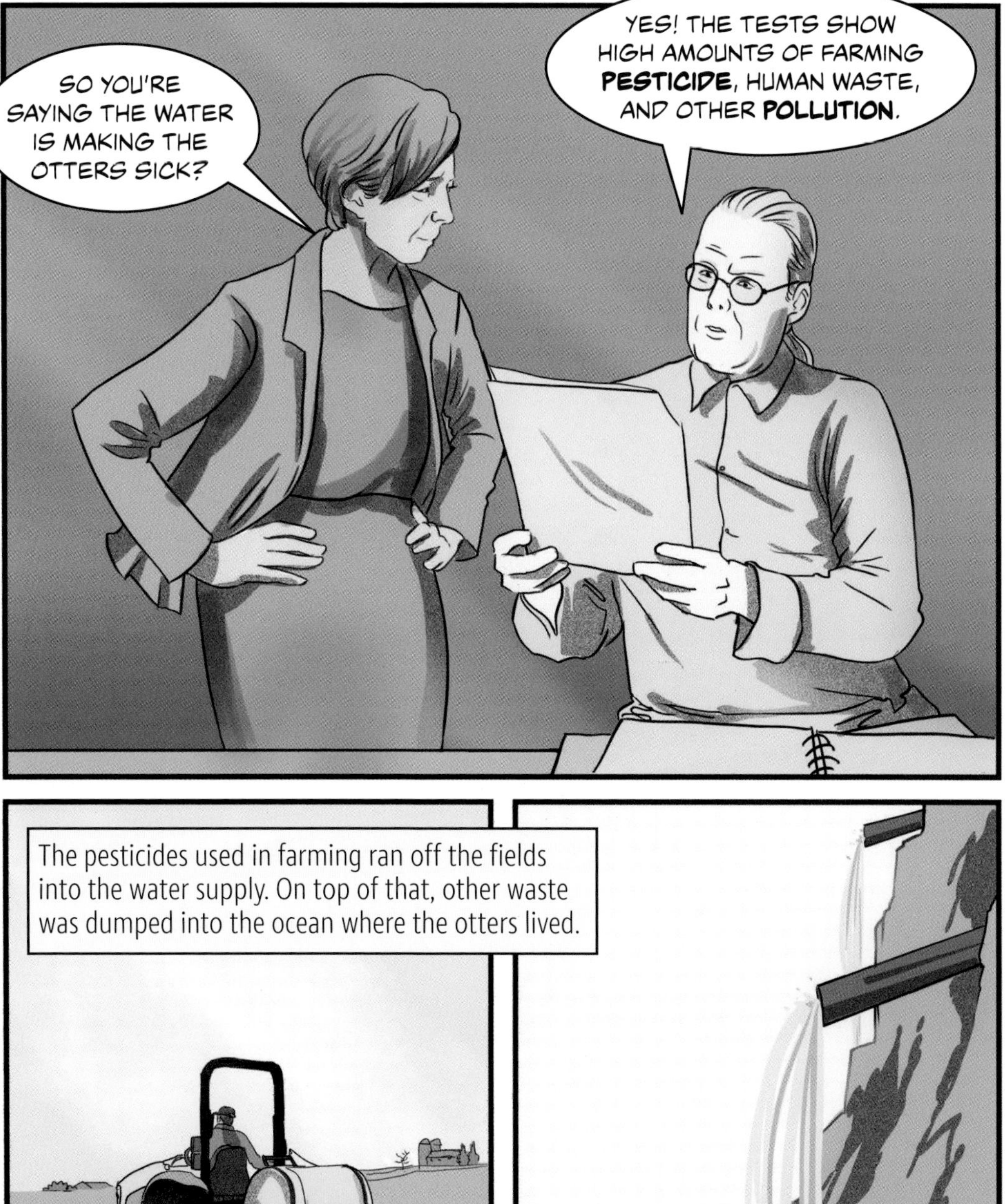
SO YOU'RE SAYING THE WATER IS MAKING THE OTTERS SICK?
YES! THE TESTS SHOW HIGH AMOUNTS OF FARMING PESTICIDE, HUMAN WASTE, AND OTHER POLLUTION.
The pesticides used in farming ran off the fields into the water supply. On top of that, other waste was dumped into the ocean where the otters lived.

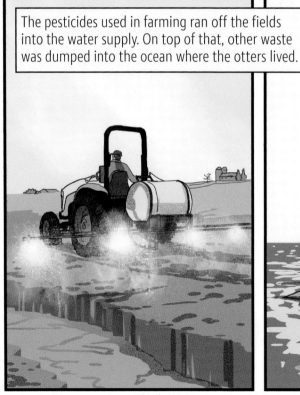

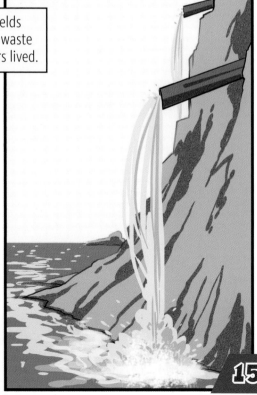

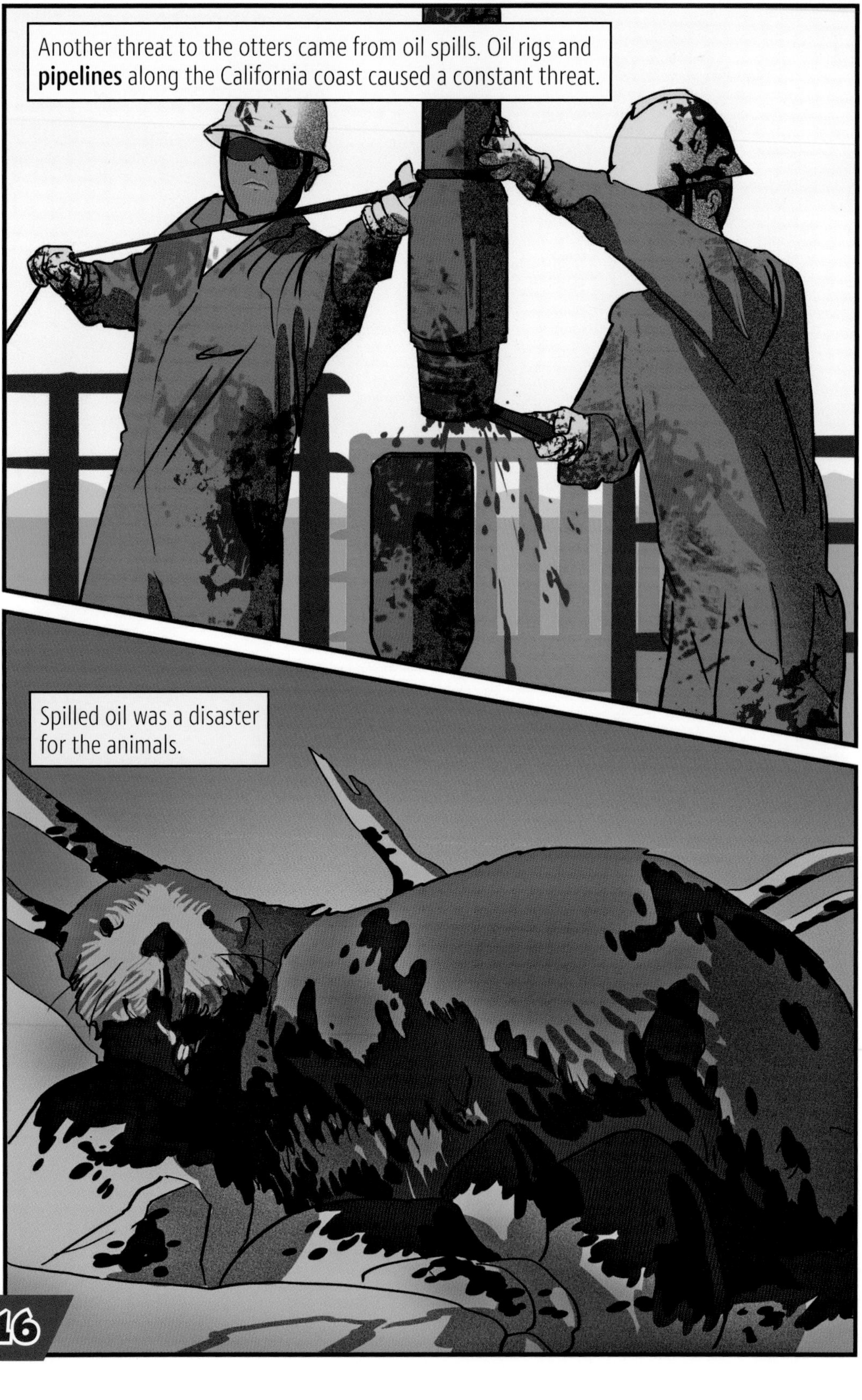
Another threat to the otters came from oil spills. Oil rigs and **pipelines** along the California coast caused a constant threat.
Spilled oil was a disaster for the animals.

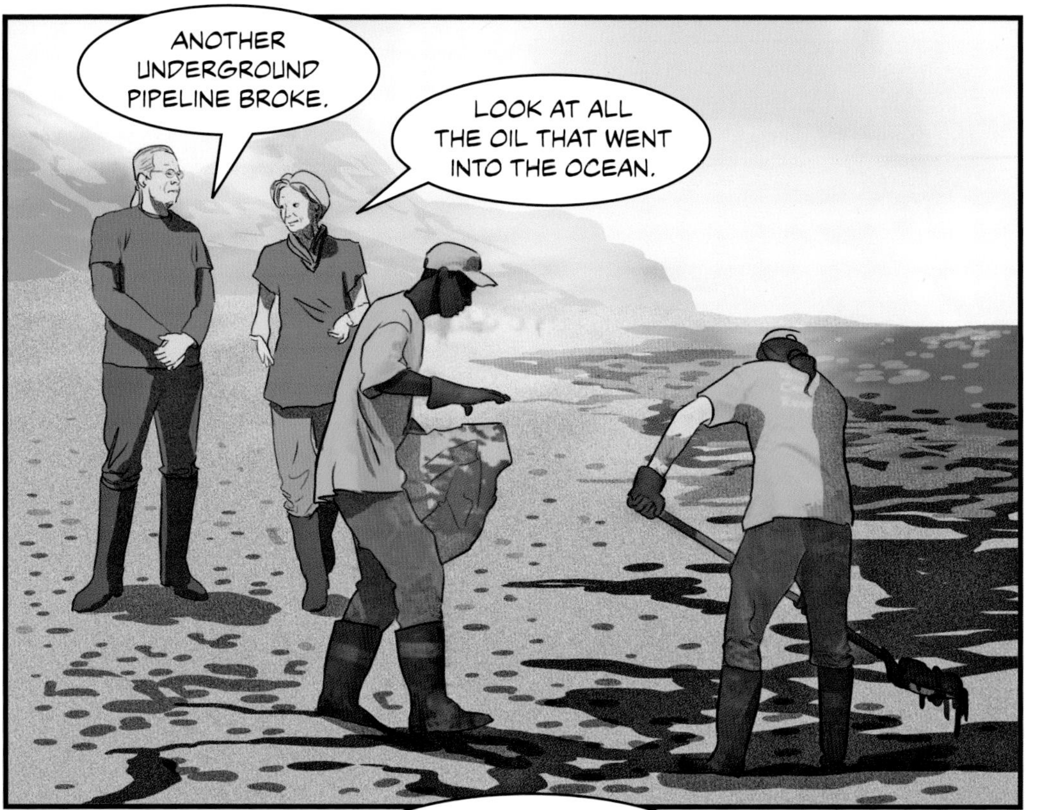
ANOTHER UNDERGROUND PIPELINE BROKE.
LOOK AT ALL THE OIL THAT WENT INTO THE OCEAN.

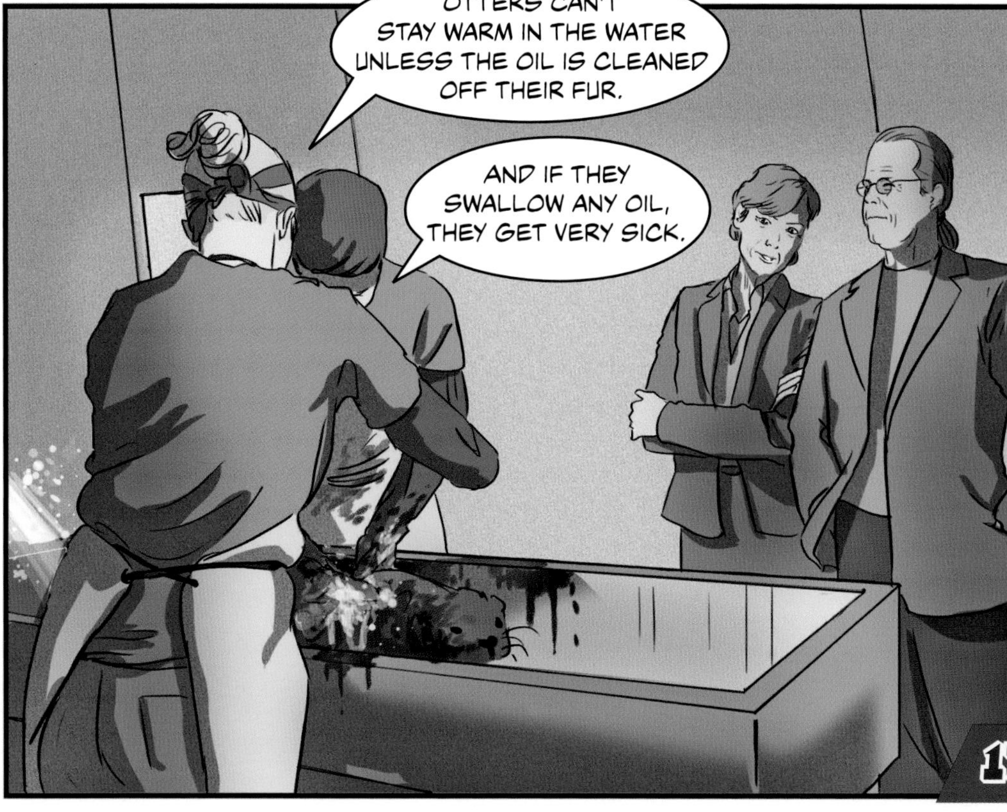
OTTERS CAN'T STAY WARM IN THE WATER UNLESS THE OIL IS CLEANED OFF THEIR FUR.
AND IF THEY SWALLOW ANY OIL, THEY GET VERY SICK.

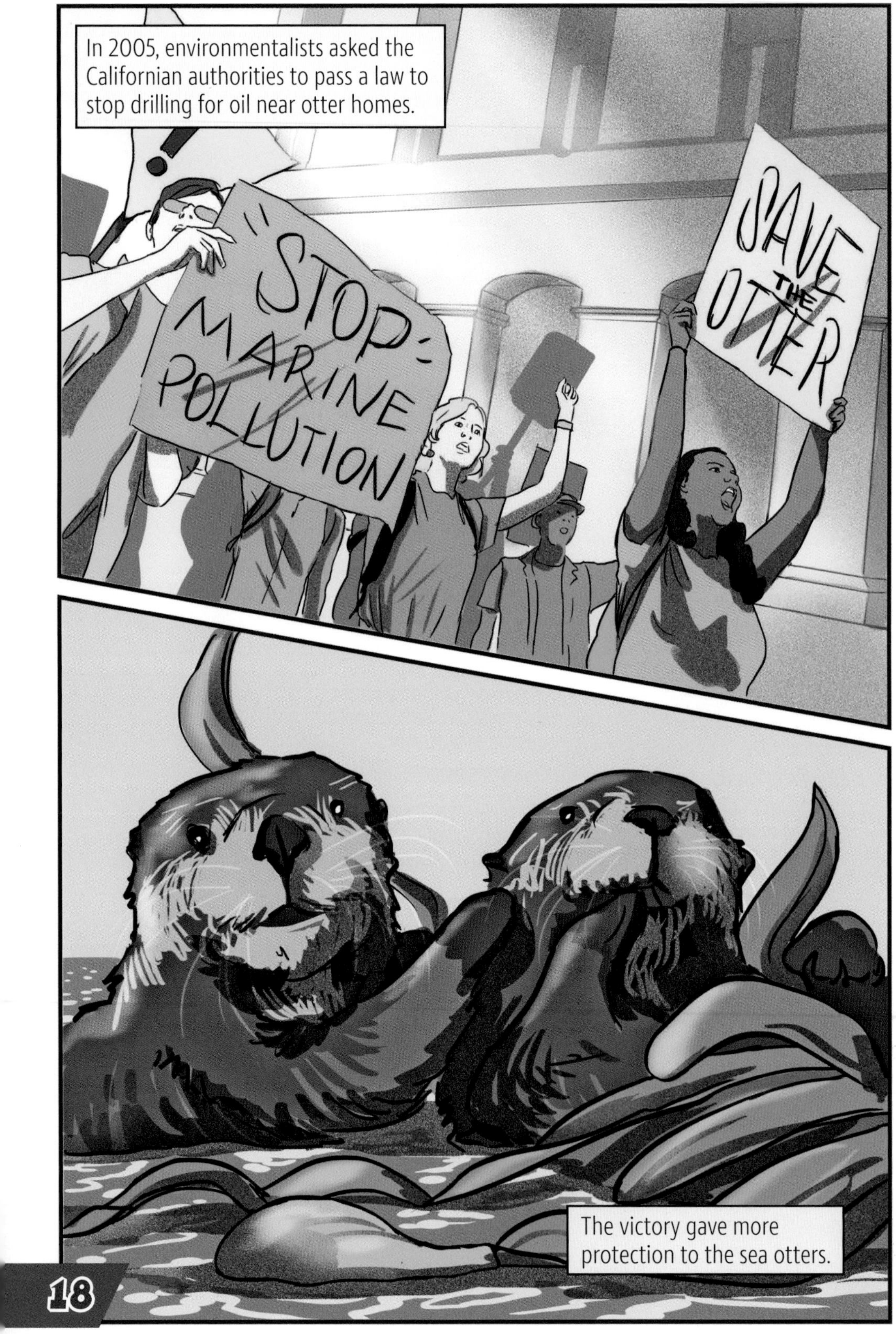
In 2005, environmentalists asked the Californian authorities to pass a law to stop drilling for oil near otter homes.
STOP MARINE POLLUTION
SAVE THE OTTER
The victory gave more protection to the sea otters.

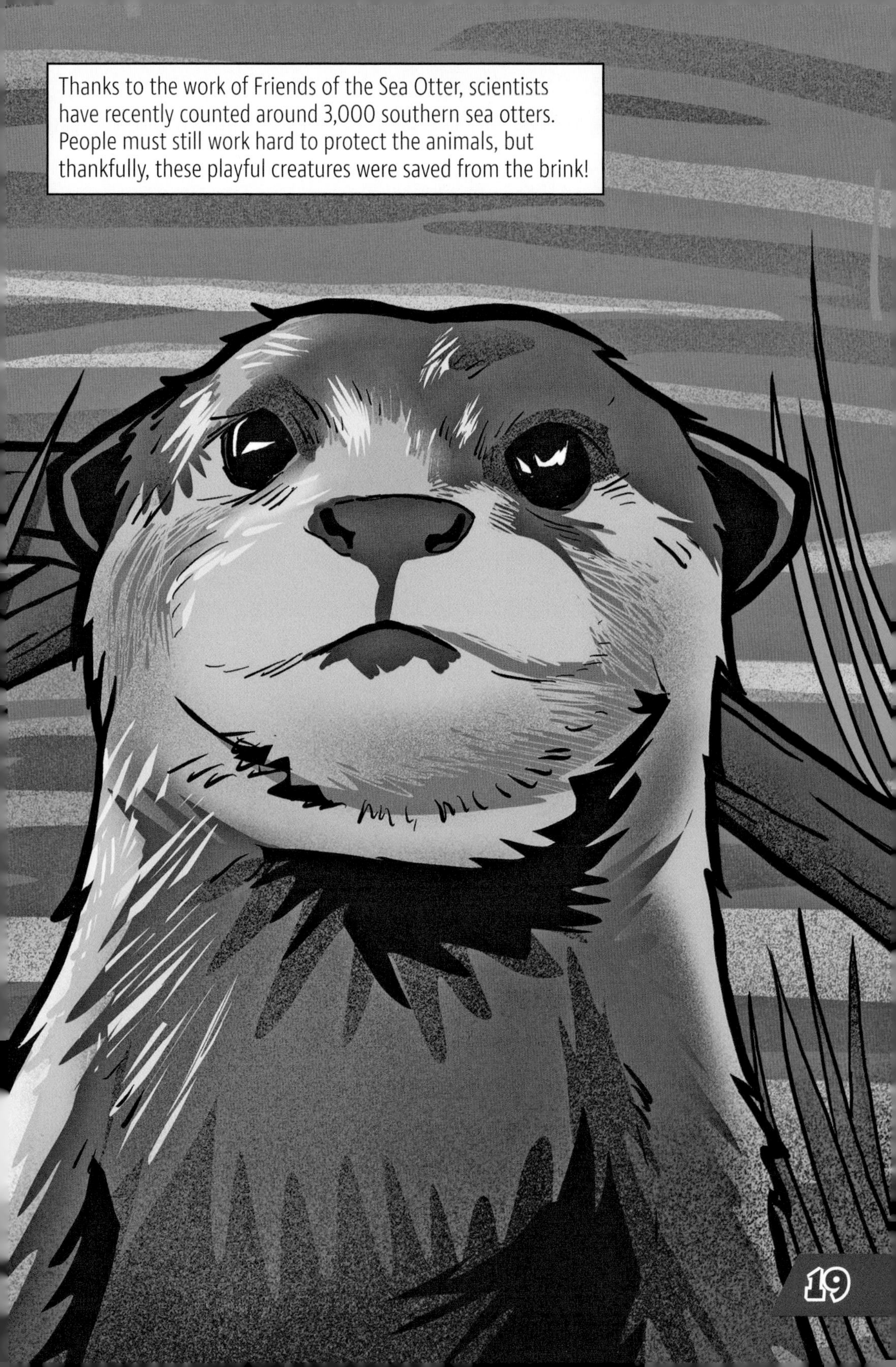
Thanks to the work of Friends of the Sea Otter, scientists have recently counted around 3,000 southern sea otters. People must still work hard to protect the animals, but thankfully, these playful creatures were saved from the brink!

SOUTHERN SEA OTTER FACTS

In 1973, the government passed the **Endangered Species** Act. This law protects animals and plants that are in danger of dying out. Activities such as hunting, capturing, harming, or collecting endangered species are illegal under this law.

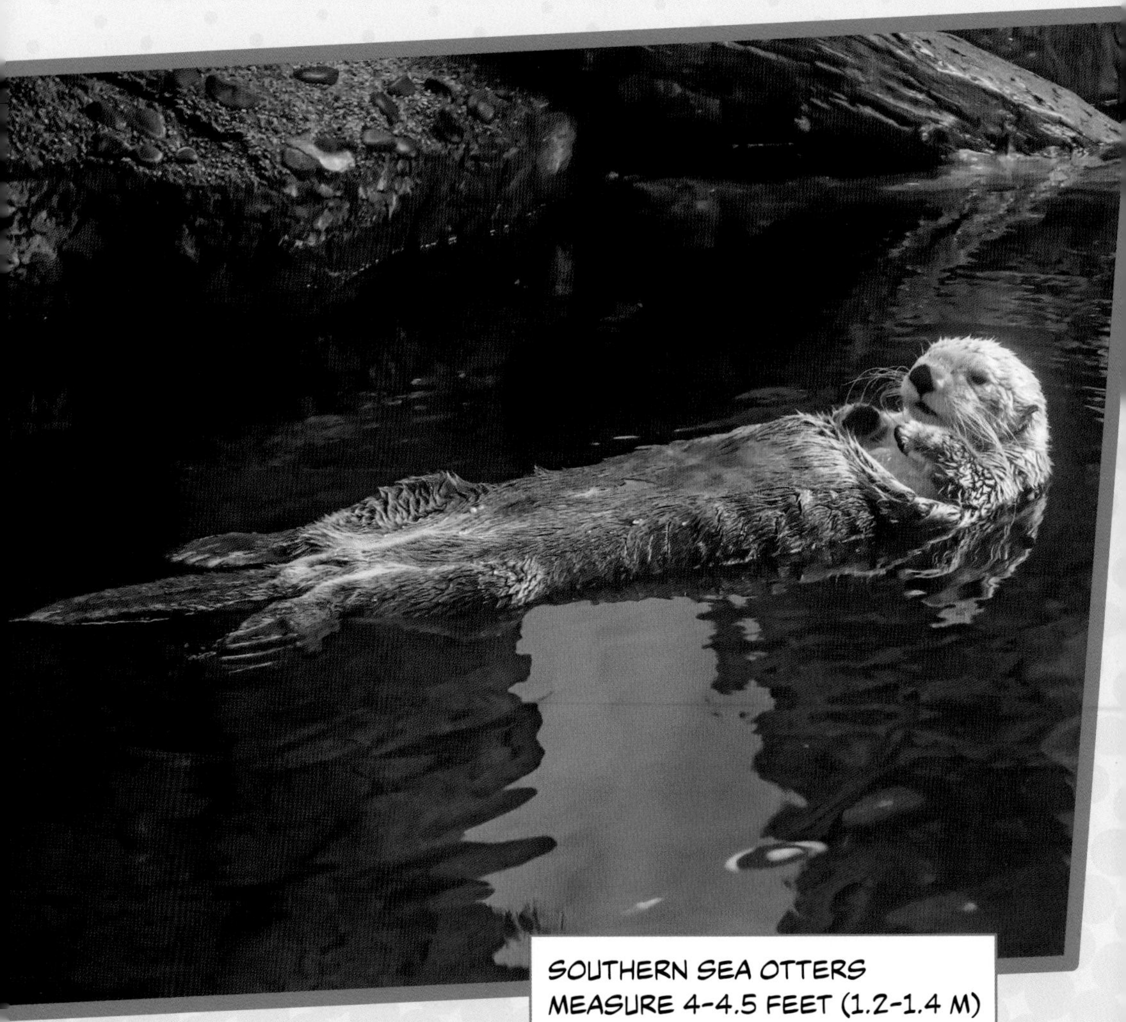

SOUTHERN SEA OTTERS MEASURE 4–4.5 FEET (1.2–1.4 M) FROM NOSE TO TAIL.

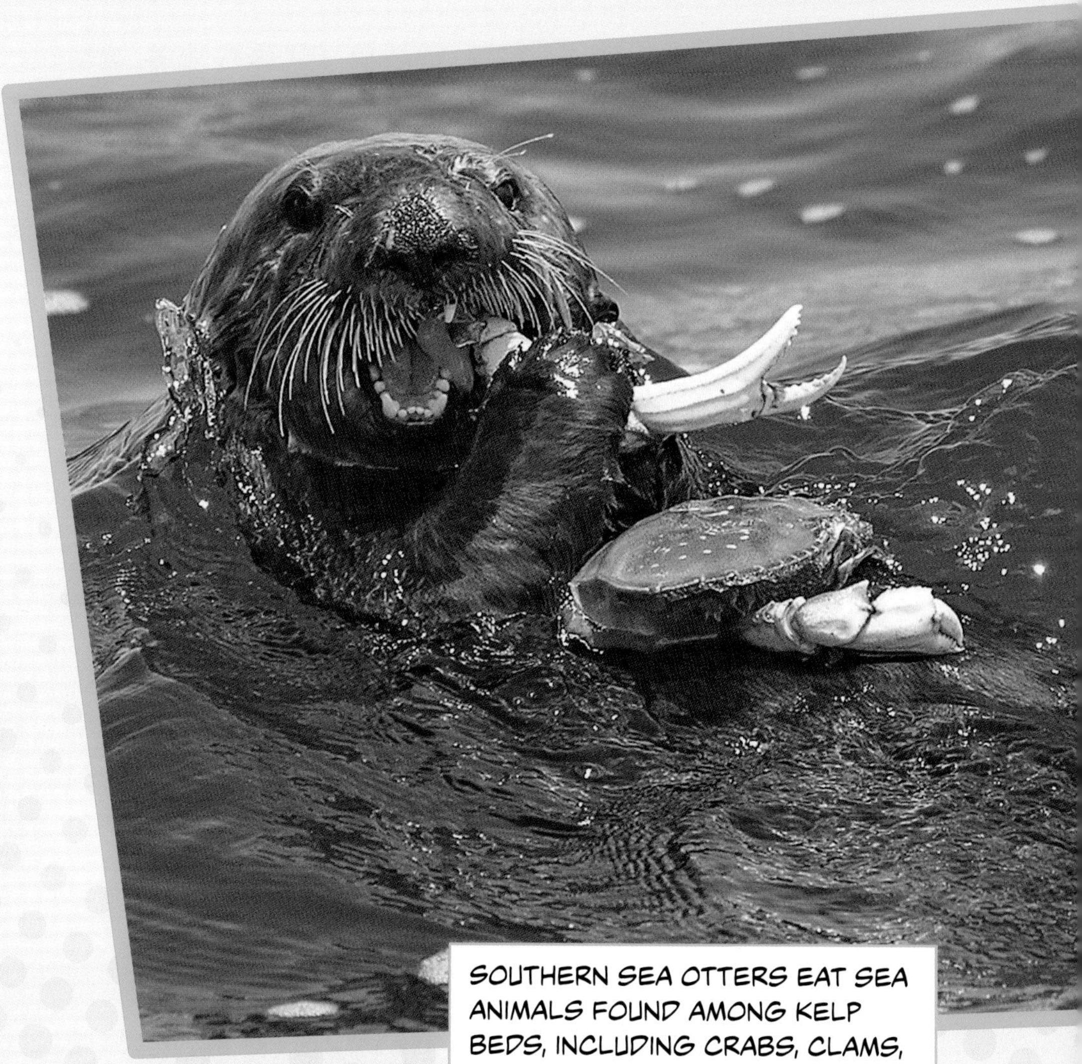

SOUTHERN SEA OTTERS EAT SEA ANIMALS FOUND AMONG KELP BEDS, INCLUDING CRABS, CLAMS, OCTOPUSES, AND SEA URCHINS.

The southern sea otter was listed as threatened under the Endangered Species Act in 1977.

There still aren't as many sea otters as there once were, but this act helped some. In 1700, there were up to 16,000 otters in the wild. Today, there are around 3,000.

OTHER MARINE MAMMALS IN DANGER

Southern sea otters are returning from the brink, but there are still other marine mammals in danger.

BLUE WHALES

Blue whales live in every ocean in the world. There are between 5,000 and 10,000 adult blue whales alive today. But they are in danger from hunting, getting caught in fishing nets, and pollution. To help protect the whales, many countries have agreed to make whale hunting illegal.

BLUE WHALES ARE THE LARGEST ANIMALS ON EARTH.

THERE ARE FEWER THAN 700 ADULT HAWAIIAN MONK SEALS LEFT IN THE WORLD.

HAWAIIAN MONK SEALS

Hawaiian monk seals live around the Hawaiian Islands in the Pacific Ocean. The seals are in danger from fishing nets, pollution, and disease. They are also eaten by **predators**, such as sharks. Scientists are trying to make sure that the animals' habitat is both clean and safe from predators.

GLOSSARY

biologist a scientist who studies plants or animals

breed to produce young

declining falling in number

endangered species a group of animals in danger of dying out

environmentalists people who work to protect plants and animals

extinct died out

habitat where a plant or animal normally lives

illegal against the law

keystone species a species that has a very large impact on its ecosystem

marine mammals mammals that live in the sea

pesticide a poisonous chemical used to kill insects and other pests on plants

pipelines systems of pipes that move oil over long distances

pollution substances that harm the environment

population the total number of a kind of animal living in a place

predators animals that hunt and eat other animals

refuge a place that provides shelter or protection

survive to continue to exist despite threats

INDEX

breed 11
Endangered Species Act 20–21
environmentalists 4, 18
food 10, 13
Friends of the Sea Otter 7–8,
  13, 19
hunted 8–9, 20, 22

kelp 13, 21
marine mammals 8, 22
oil 16–18
pollution 15, 22
San Nicolas Island 10, 12
Sharpe, Howard 4, 7

READ MORE

Emminizer, Theresa. *What If Sea Otters Disappeared? (Life Without Animals)*. New York: Gareth Stevens Publishing, 2020.

Gish, Ashley. *Sea Otters (X-Books: Marine Mammals)*. Mankato, MN: Creative Education, 2019.

Kenney, Karen Latchana. *Saving the Sea Otter (Great Animal Comebacks)*. Minneapolis: Jump! Inc. 2019.

LEARN MORE ONLINE

1. Go to **www.factsurfer.com**

2. Enter **"Otter Comeback"** into the search box.

3. Click on the cover of this book to see a list of websites.